Kate Finds a Caterpillar

A Book about the Life Cycle of a Butterfly

BY KERRY DINMONT

Published by The Child's World®
1980 Lookout Drive • Mankato, MN 56003-1705
800-599-READ • www.childsworld.com

Photographs ©: Cathy Keifer/Shutterstock Images, cover, 1, 8;
Shutterstock Images, 3, 4–5; Marsha Mood/Shutterstock Images, 7;
Jacob Hamblin/Shutterstock Images, 11; Steven Russell Smith Photos/
Shutterstock Images, 12, 15, 16; Perry Correll/Shutterstock Images, 19;
Brandon Alms/Shutterstock Images, 20

Design Elements: Ambient Ideas/Shutterstock Images

ISBN 9781503820159
LCCN 2016960935

Printed in the United States of America
PA02339

Today, Kate finds a caterpillar.

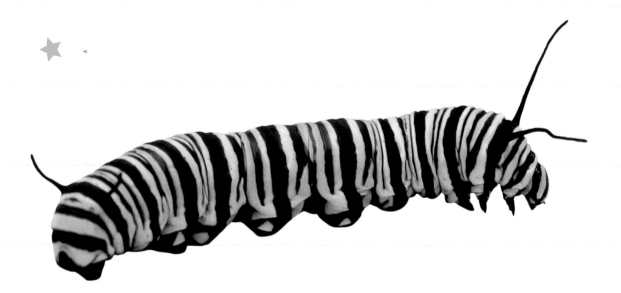

What will it become?

Kate plays at the park.
She finds a caterpillar
on a leaf.

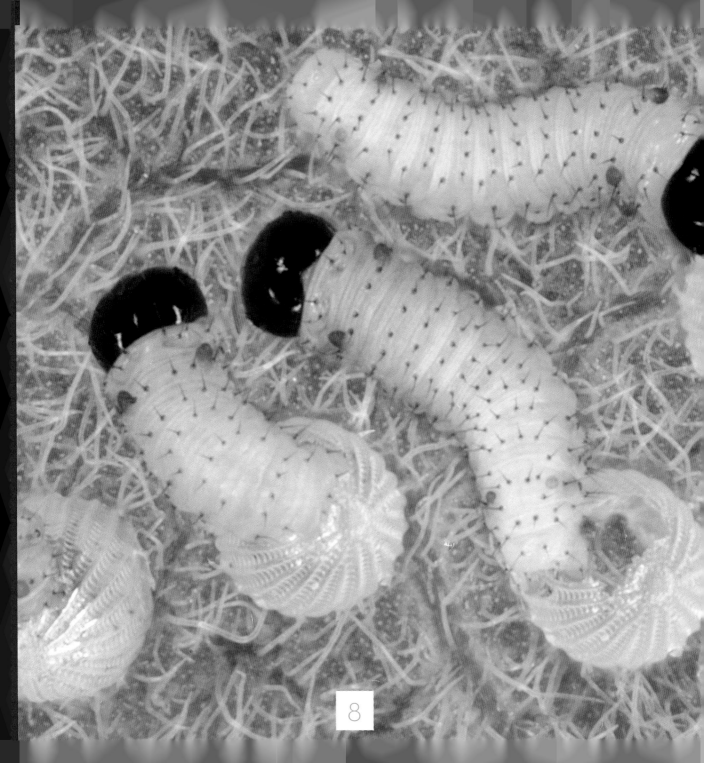

8

Kate learned about caterpillars in school. Caterpillars begin as eggs. They **hatch**.

The caterpillar eats leaves. It grows bigger.

12

Soon it hangs from a twig. The caterpillar is in a shell. The shell is called a **chrysalis**.

The chrysalis does not move. But the caterpillar changes inside.

15

Then, a butterfly comes out! It has colorful wings.

The butterfly will lay its own eggs. The **cycle** starts again.

20

Where have you seen
a caterpillar?

Words to Know

chrysalis (KRIS-uh-lis) A chrysalis is the hard case that protects a butterfly while it changes. A chrysalis hangs from a branch.

cycle (SYE-kuhl) A cycle is a series of events that repeat in the same order. A butterfly begins its life cycle as an egg.

hatch (HACH) To hatch is to break out of an egg. Caterpillars hatch out of eggs.

Extended Learning Activities

1 Butterflies come in many different colors. What kinds of butterflies have you seen?

2 How do you think a butterfly gets out of a chrysalis?

3 Can you think of any other animals that hatch from eggs?

To Learn More

Books

Delano, Marfe Ferguson. *Butterflies*.
Washington, DC: National Geographic Society, 2014.

Edwards, Roberta. *Flight of the Butterflies*.
New York, NY: Grosset & Dunlap, 2010.

Wallace, Karen. *Born to Be a Butterfly*.
London, UK: Dorling Kindersley, 2010.

Web Sites

Visit our Web site for links about butterflies:
childsworld.com/links

Note to Parents, Teachers, and Librarians: We routinely verify our Web links to make sure they are safe and active sites. So encourage your readers to check them out!

About the Author

Kerry Dinmont is a children's book author who enjoys art and nature. She lives in Montana with her two Norwegian elkhounds.